To Katja, I do hope you en[joy the] story. Such a f[...]
Mum xx

This copy of The Parcel belongs to:

The author, illustrator and field mice Rachel, Jack and Uncle Olivier all hope you enjoy their story.

Michael R Beddard   Rebecca Yoxall

ACKNOWLEDGEMENTS

Very many people have helped with the creation of this book. I am very grateful to them all, and especially to my sister and editor Pam Beddard; to my mother, Edith Beddard for a lifetime of love and support; to my eagle-eyed proof-reader Tony Coll; to my nephew Dominic and friend Linda for crash courses in Spanish and to Don Anderson, Caroline Cliffe and Mrs Smith for their all-round encouragement. Special thanks are also due to Vanessa Duffy and the children of Norley Primary School, Cheshire, for test-reading the story and providing some very useful feedback. **MRB**

NO MICE WERE INJURED IN THE MAKING OF THIS STORY

First published in Great Britain by Michael R Beddard, July 2013,
Northwich, Cheshire, CW9 8DA.

beautybankpublishing@gmail.com

© Copyright: Michael R Beddard

ISBN 978-0-9573022-1-1

All rights reserved. No part of this publication may be reproduced, distributed, or transmitted in any form or by any means, including photocopying, recording, or other electronic or mechanical methods, without the prior written permission of the publisher and illustrator.

www.beautybankpublishing.com

Printed in the UK
THINKPRINT
01606 784567
sales@thinkprint.co.uk

Introduction

A hallmark of the TALES FROM BEAUTY BANK stories is that each is built around an act of kindness by characters who want to make someone else's tricky situation better. The stories speak especially strongly to me because, through my job as Ambassador of the Carers Trust, I meet real people demonstrating this type of kindness every day.

The paths which lead to a person becoming a carer vary greatly and it isn't always an easy role, as Mike the author of this book and a carer himself knows very well. But the journey nearly always starts with the realisation that not everyone can manage alone and that by giving help where help is needed, we can make a big and positive difference, both to the life of an individual and to the overall sense of goodness in the world.

In this story, we find out what happens when field mice Rachel, Jack and their Uncle Olivier find themselves at the heart of a mystery. An important parcel is missing. Can the little mice and their wildlife friends find it, and return it, in time to save a very important day in the life of the village?

I am delighted to find that an act of kindness is at the core of this story and very much hope that you enjoy it, too.

Carole Cochrane CBE, DL
Ambassador of the Carers Trust   www.carers.org

High above the cotton wool clouds, amidst the sky so blue there's a magical place where unwritten stories live. Close your eyes, let your imagination run free, and write down what you see.

MRB

Tales from Beauty Bank

THE PARCEL

by

Michael R Beddard

Illustrated

by

Rebecca Yoxall

This book is dedicated to:

Kevin Ian Jones
of
Beauty Bank

To the outsider's eye Beauty Bank is as ordinary as any other quiet and pretty Cheshire village.

But 'ordinary' is hardly ever how it appears to the family of field mice – Rachel, her younger brother Jack and their Uncle Olivier – who live in the riverside meadow just outside of Beauty Bank.

For them every new morning brings the promise of an extraordinary adventure just waiting to happen.

On this morning, however, adventure seems far way. Spring is in the air, the sun is shining and Rachel is sitting on the riverbank, fascinated by the movements of a leaf being carried in the sparkling water as it ripples along like liquid glass.

There is a small pebble island in the middle of the river and the leaf is dancing around it like a ballerina, caught in a fast little stream threading through the stones.

The spell is only broken when suddenly the leaf escapes the island's current and is whisked downstream and out of sight.

Alert now, Rachel turns her head to look across the wild flower-filled meadow which her Uncle Olivier calls his garden.

Screwing up her eyes against the sun, Rachel looks towards her little brother, Jack, running near the hedge in a very strange manner.

"What is that silly boy up to now?" she smiled, as Jack raced forwards and back, holding one paw tight in front of him and regularly smacking the air behind him with the other.

"Ah! Is he being a cowboy on a horse?" she guessed, and then laughed out loud when he proved her right by spinning an imaginary lasso above his head so wildly, he almost fell out of his make-believe saddle.

She was just about to call to him "Whoa, pardner" when a loud clatter, thud, and a cry broke the silence for her.

It came from the old sandstone bridge and was followed by a large cloud of papers fluttering high into the air, and the sounds of a very unhappy person grunting, groaning, moaning and muttering from underneath them.

Sitting higher, Rachel discovered the groans were coming from a postman, sprawled across his fallen-down bike, with envelopes and packages raining down all around him.

After a short time, the postman stood and started wagging an angry finger at the large pothole which had tumbled him, his bike and his satchel full of mail to the ground.

As soon as she knew the postman wasn't injured, Rachel couldn't resist a giggle at his grumbles as he collected the scattered mail, stuffed the items back into his red postbag and picked up his bike before wobbling away with one last angry look at the pothole.

"Hey, sis!" shouted Jack, galloping up from across the meadow, dragging a very long twig. "Did you see the snowstorm?"

His sister laughed. "It wasn't snow, stupid. Snow only falls in winter. The stuff in the air was because the postman came off his bike, sending everything in his bag flying. But what are you up to? What's the stick for?"

"Sorry," replied Jack. "I would tell you. But it's for a very important, hush-hush, top secret, job, so... I can't." Rachel twitched her whiskers. "Huh! More daft mischief, I suppose. Well, don't come running to me if it all goes wrong."

Jack did his best to look as if he'd never ever dreamed of making mischief as he sidled slowly away towards the hedgerow next to the stone bridge, dragging his twig behind him.

Once there, he looked quickly to his left, to his right and back over his shoulder to make sure no one was watching and then put Operation Twig into action.

For his first go, he prodded it hard at the hedge but soon discovered the twig couldn't reach in as far as he needed. So, he tried again – this time stretching out until he was balancing most of his weight on the spindly stick.

Success seemed near when – CRACK – the twig broke, tumbling him into the ditch below.

"Hrumph," he said, picking himself up and brushing himself down. "Perhaps this is a Top Secret Mission best done by two."

Trotting back to his sister, he put on what he hoped was his most appealing face and said: "Rachel. If I were to tell you about my top secret mission, would you help me with it... please?"

Rachel was, of course, very keen to know what her brother was doing but also determined not to appear over-eager. So, instead of replying straightaway, she counted to ten in her head and yawned before replying: "Oh, all right, I suppose. What IS the big secret, then?"

"Well, you know I was playing cowboys and Indians over there by the stone bridge"....

Rachel interrupted: "Who with?"

"No one" replied Jack. "I was on my own. So, anyway...."

"But that's stupid. How can you play cowboys and Indians alone? Cowboys, right? Indians, right? It needs at least two."

"Doh", said Jack. "I was the cowboy and the Indians were hiding, and that's the point. The Indians must have been holed up on the other side of the bridge – and with some space aliens, too – because... and this is the secret... they sent a UFO to beam me up..."

Jack hadn't noticed that Rachel was, by now, fighting hard not to laugh. He simply carried on with his story.

"Of course, I was too fast – dodged out of the way as quick as a flash, and the UFO crash-landed, smack in the hedge. And that's the mission – to get to the UFO and find what – or who – is inside."

"So," said Rachel. "Let me get this straight. You want me to help you find an Unidentified Flying Object that was launched by an imaginary band of Indians – and aliens – during a make-believe battle, fought just by you, on a horse that wasn't there?"

"But the UFO is there, I tell you," Jack protested. "It came flying over the bridge and dropped into the hedge. I've tried getting at it with a stick but it's too high up and... well... my twig broke and I... erm... fell in the ditch."

"So, what's it like, then? A flying saucer?" asked Rachel mockingly.

"No. Like I said, it's a UFO – a flying object that's unidentified. I reckon it must be a new design. It's square and brown, with stuff tied around it and funny squiggles on the front. But see for yourself. I'll show you!"

"Okay, bro, but something tells me your UFO isn't quite what you think – and that we're going to need Uncle Olivier's help. So let's go and see if he's... ahem... free".

With Rachel leading, the two mice ran quickly to their home – a cosy hollow inside a fallen oak tree, close to the river bank. Inside, Jack and Rachel found Uncle Olivier busy enjoying his very favourite pastime of all: sleeping.

Rachel nodded to Jack. "The usual?" he asked. "The usual" she agreed – at which Jack scampered close to his uncle's left ear and in a very loud voice yelled: "Wakey, wakey!!!"

Uncle Olivier sat bolt upright immediately, with an "Oh!", "My whiskers!" "What's happening?" and "Who's there?" before realising his nephew was grinning cheerfully nearby.

"Oh Jack!" protested Uncle Olivier. "How many times do I have to tell you, not to do that? Think of my heart, dear boy. Think of my blood pressure!"

"Sorry, Uncle Olivier," said Rachel. "But we need your help with a mission."

Uncle Olivier rubbed the sleep from his eyes and looked fondly at the young mice. "A mission, is it? Well, then, we'd best investigate. You know our family's motto by now: 'onwards or upwards'."

Outside, Uncle Olivier stretched out and breathed deeply. "What a beautiful sunny morning. Just look at the bright blue of that sky. And what does that little cloud remind you of, Jack? A dragon, perhaps?"

By now, the mice were crossing the meadow towards the bridge with Rachel explaining the morning's events to her uncle.

Jack was so busy looking at cloud shapes above that he missed the old tree root poking out of the ground below, tripped, and – whoops – fell flat on his face near the hedge.

Rachel sniffed. "Typical". But Uncle Olivier just peered across his nephew's body into the thorns and blossoms of the hedge, looking puzzled.

"Are you sure this is the place, Jack? Only I can't see anything unusual in the hedge at all".

"Lie down here next to me, then", said Jack, picking up the remains of his broken twig to use as a pointer. "There. See? Buried deep in the middle."

"Well, I never", said Uncle Olivier. "I wouldn't have spotted that on my own in a million years, Jack".

"See, Rachel," said Jack, smugly. "I told you a UFO landed."

"Yes," said Rachel, even more smugly. "But, you also said the object was launched by space aliens but I'd say that what we're looking at is a small parcel, wrapped in brown paper and tied with string".

"Now, children, don't squabble," said Uncle Olivier. "You're both right. It is a parcel but it's a mystery object as well. What is it doing in our hedge, I wonder? It really is most odd".

"And will there be an odd-looking space creature inside?" asked Jack, hopefully.

"Unlikely, brother, but there's only one way to find out", said practical Rachel. "We'll have to get the parcel out of the hedge and have a look".

"I tried that", retorted Jack, "with my prodding stick."

"So you did", sniggered Rachel. "But fell into the ditch, instead".

"Children, children", said Uncle Olivier. "This is no time for arguments. We need to fully assess the situation so that we can draw up an action plan."

To start, they began walking the full length of the ditch under the hedgerow. But, soon, only Uncle Olivier was 'thinking'.

Jack was investigating a rusted water trough riddled with interesting holes, while Rachel was practising tightrope-walking, using a long loose tangle from a ball of old baling twine.

Suddenly, Uncle Olivier snapped to attention and called: "That's it! Rachel! Hurry now. Bring that twine here".

Unfortunately, Rachel had just reached a tricky point in her tightrope routine. Startled by Uncle Olivier's shout, she wobbled, lost her balance, and then fell from the twine, landing flat – splat – in a fresh cow pat!

This made Jack laugh so hard his sides ached and even Uncle Olivier gave a broad grin – until, that is, Rachel picked herself up, glared fiercely at them both and snapped "Oh grow up!" before stomping to the water's edge to get clean.

Rachel was still sounding cross when she ordered Jack to help her to gather up the roll of baling twine and carry it over to where Uncle Olivier was sitting, under a shady elderflower tree.

But by then, all the walking, talking, exploring and thinking had tired out the older mouse so that when the little ones returned, he was already snoozing.

"The usual, again?" Jack asked Rachel. "Not this time, Jack. Let him be. We could do with a bit of rest ourselves.".

It was a lovely day, and as a warm breeze ruffled Rachel's fur, a ladybird settled on a bluebell beside her.

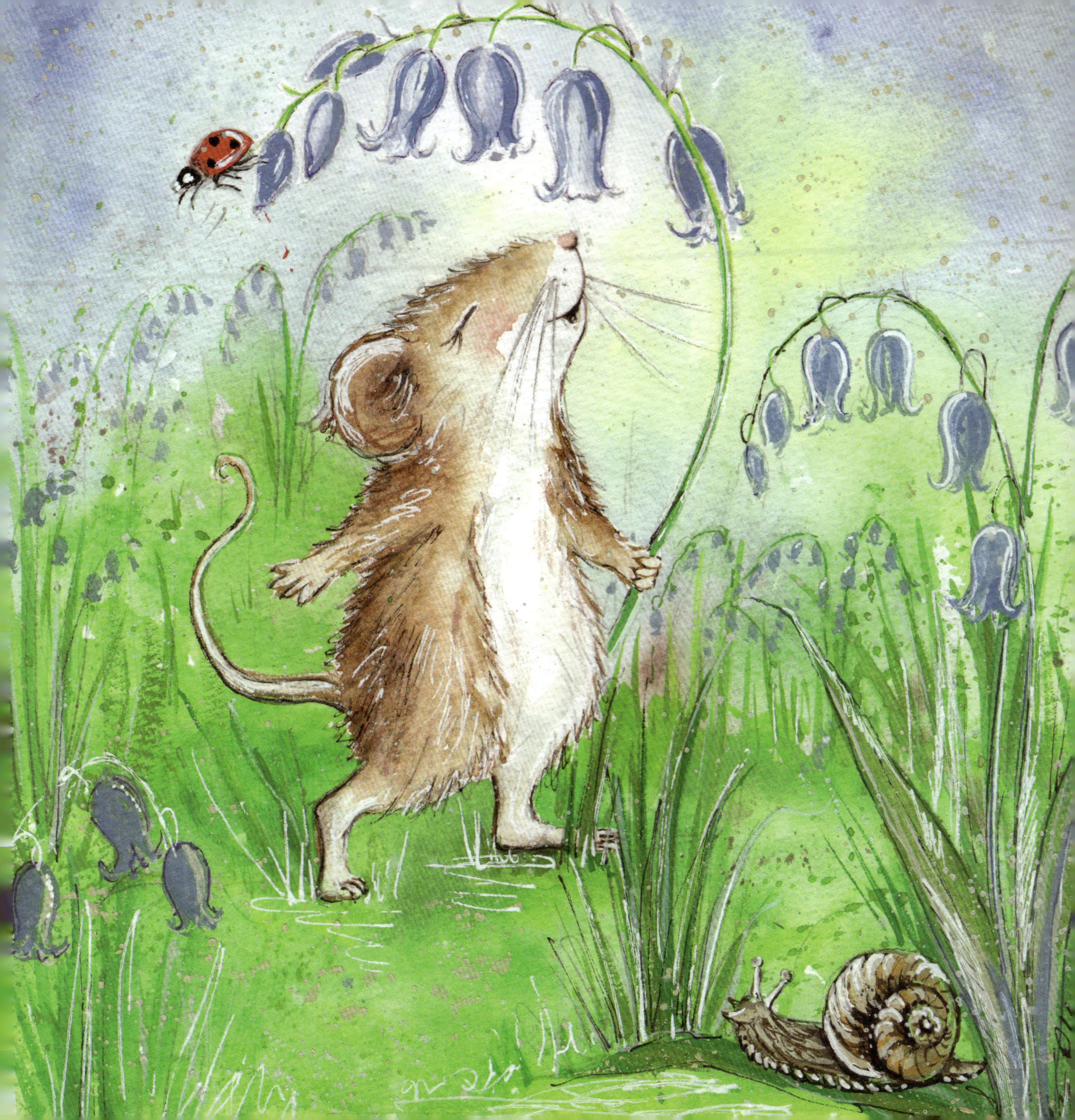

Keeping very still, Rachel studied the dots on its red and black back until, as quickly as it had landed, another gust of air carried the ladybird on and away.

For once, Jack was also sitting quietly and as Rachel looked across she thought there was a teardrop in his eye. "Jack? Is everything all right? You haven't hurt yourself, have you?"

"No," he sniffled. "I'm okay. It's just.... well... I was thinking about Mummy and Daddy, and wishing they were here. Daddy would definitely know what to do about the hedge and the parcel and... sniff... I do miss them."

"Me, too, Jack", said Rachel, sitting beside him and holding him close. "But at least we know they are safe and well. Remember what Uncle Olivier told us – that Mickey the water rat's cousin, Walter, saw them on a river boat eating a jam and cream scone from a Women's Institute outing?" She promised: "They're just waiting for another boat to come in our direction and then we'll all be back together again."

"I do hope so," replied Jack, a little cheerier. "And it was very funny, wasn't it, when they got on the river cruiser and the lady saw them on the gang-plank, screamed and fell in the river?"

"No, Jack, it wasn't even a bit funny. I've never been so embarrassed in my life. All those people jumping about shrieking 'Mice, mice'. No wonder Mummy grabbed Daddy and hid.

It should be a lesson for you. If Daddy hadn't gone where he shouldn't, they wouldn't have got stuck on the boat and left us. But I promise, it will all work out well in the end."

"Work out well in the end, eh?" Uncle Olivier woke suddenly. "Does this mean you've guessed my clever plan?"

"Oh, no, Uncle, we're really keen to hear it," said Rachel brightly and loudly, before moving closer to her uncle and whispering. "Jack's been a bit upset – about missing Mum and Dad. I'm hoping your plan will give him something else to think about."

Then, in a voice loud enough for Jack to hear, she added: "Here's the twine you wanted, Uncle. I was hoping it would do as a skipping rope but it won't. It's too light. I really need string."

"Ah, yes, twine," said Uncle Olivier. "An idea with twine! Oh, dear. I know I had it clear a moment ago. But what was it? Oh, yes. I remember now. Nuts!"

"Nuts?" repeated the children; giving each other a look which showed they were both wondering if their uncle was describing himself.

"Yes, nuts," said Uncle Olivier, firmly. "We're going to need some extra help with this job but, first, you need to run back to our food store and bring me as many peanuts as you can carry. And a small piece of silver foil."

At this, he closed his eyes. "While you are gone, I'll sit here to... er... mull over the plan, my dears." And before the children had taken 10 steps towards their oak tree, he was already softly snoring...

Back at the food store, it took the young mice a while to work out how to carry their uncle's shopping list of peanuts and silver foil.

After much experimenting, they decided to pile the nuts on top of the shiny sheet of silver foil and drag it along behind them like a sledge.

Uncle Olivier clapped when they arrived, huffing and puffing, back at his resting spot. "Wonderful! Four plump peanuts! Well done! That should definitely do the trick."

After helping them to unload the sledge, he explained: "Now we need to tear the foil up and place two nuts on one of the pieces over there, on that patch of short grass, and use the rest to wrap up these two peanuts to keep here by our feet".

Tasks completed, the children joined their uncle sitting on the tree stump, "What's next, then?" asked Jack excitedly. "Next," said Uncle Olivier grandly "We wait and we watch".

It was mid-morning in Beauty Bank and business was quiet in the village shops. So, Mrs Green took the opportunity to restock the fruit and vegetables on the display on the paved area just outside of her shop: Village Provisions.

As she tidied and swept, she was surprised to hear raised voices coming from the Post Office next door. And, being a very... ahem... curious person, she decided that the part of the display which most needed a tidy-up was the spot nearest to the argument!

It was hard to make out exactly what was being said, particularly with Alfie, her cat, weaving around her legs and mewing for attention... But what Mrs Green did gather is that there had been a worrying enquiry from one of the village's most important residents and it was all because a parcel he was expecting had not arrived.

As a result, Helen, the postmistress, was questioning Bill the postman very carefully about the parcel's whereabouts.

Mrs Green had just heard the postmistress saying: "But I most definitely gave you a parcel to deliver to Mr..." when her eavesdropping was interrupted......

Mr Buckley arrived at the shop with his collie dog Charlie and whilst he was being served, Charlie seized the moment to sniff the vegetables on display, and cock a leg on the artificial grass. And by the time Mrs Green had finished serving, she was disappointed to discover that the conversation next door had faded away.

She was just leaning on her broom thinking over what she had heard when she glanced upwards and saw a magpie landing on the roof of the post office.

"Oh dear" she thought. "What's the old saying about magpies? One for sorrow."

Up on the roof, the magpie – known as Rose to her animal friends – was admiring how the sunshine was adding a shine to her beautiful blue, green and purple-coloured feathers.

But as the church bell began to strike noon, Rose soared into the clear blue sky above the village, in search of food.

Vine Cottage was usually a good place to start. For breakfast, Mrs Johnston liked to eat hot buttered toast covered in thick marmalade and always put the crusts out afterwards onto her bird table. Rose had developed a strong liking for the shredded orange peel in the jam. In fact, there is only one other food Rose enjoys more, and that is...

A sudden noise startled Rose, sending her back into the air and onto the roof of blue bell cottage, from where she could take in the view beyond the church, across the fields towards the river.

And it was then that she saw them... two people were walking up to the old stone bridge – one on the left hand side of the lane, one, on the right; both with their heads down and both parting and prodding the roadside greenery with long walking sticks.

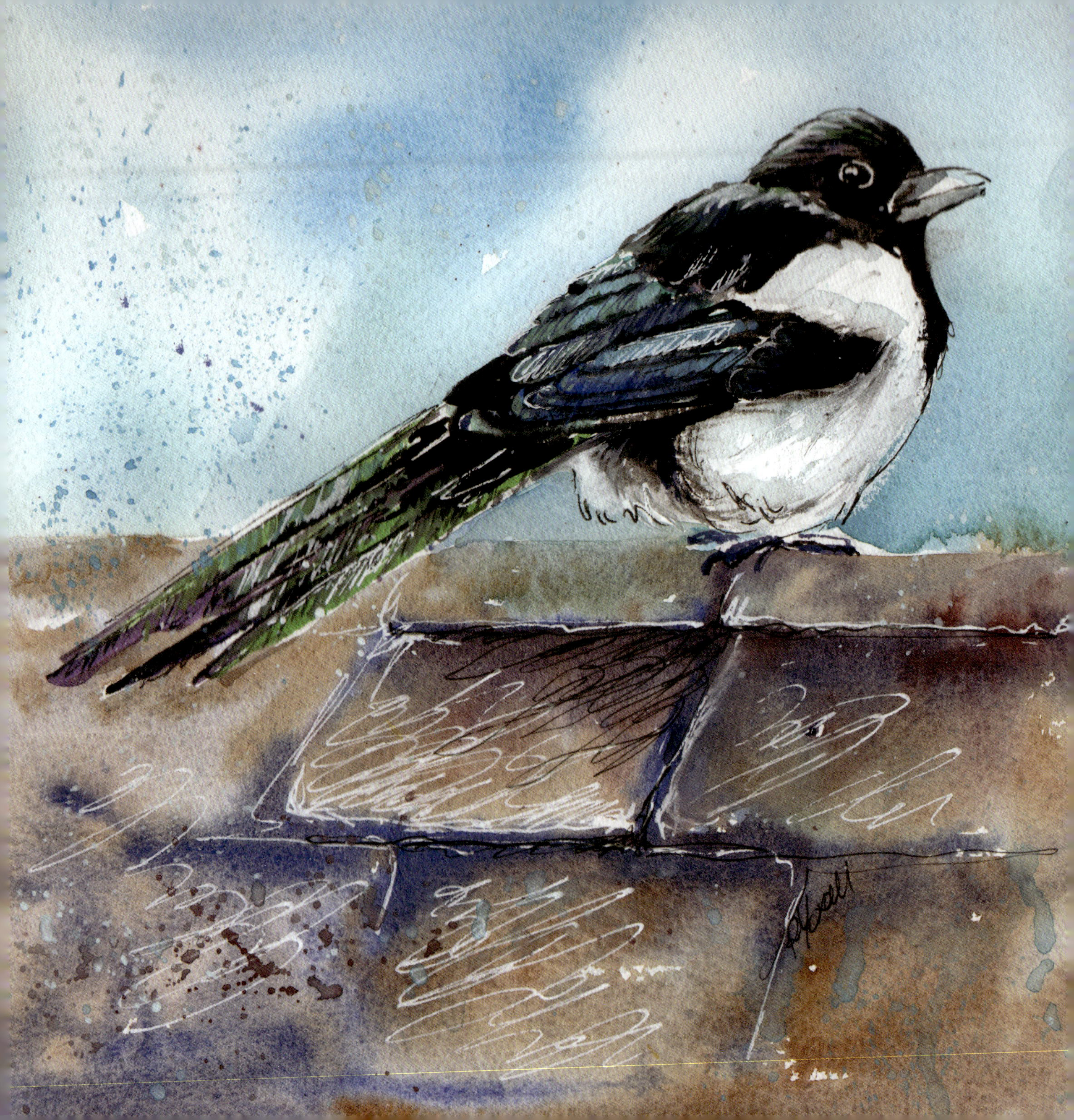

Now magpies, of course, are very inquisitive birds so Rose could not resist taking a closer look. And after landing on a fence post near to the couple, her curiosity grew even more.

"Strange", the bird thought. " It's Helen and Bill from the village Post Office – but why are they out here in the middle of the day, and what are they doing with those sticks?"

Intrigued, Rose began following the pair, hopping from fence-post to fence-post, turning her head from side to side, as magpies often do, and stopping to stare every now and again in the hope of picking up a clue.

Rose had just settled on the stone bridge when Helen called to Bill: "Show me exactly where you fell. We need to look extra carefully there".

Bill bristled with hurt: "I didn't come off my bike on purpose, Helen. It was the fault of that pot-hole! One minute I was riding along cheerfully. The next, me, the bike and the post were all sent flying. But I'm sure I collected everything up. I've been a postie long enough to know that what I deliver is often important, you know!"

Beneath the bridge, the ears of the little mice pricked up at the sound of the postman's protests.

"What's going on, now?" wondered Uncle Olivier.

"Shall I nip over and take a look?" suggested Jack.

"Yes", said Rachel, "but do try not to fall over this time!"

In reply, Jack stuck his pink tongue out at Rachel but did take more care over with his feet as he scrambled up the bank to the bridge.

As he neared the top, the voices were clearer. The lady was very upset. "I can't believe we can't find it! Mr Winstanley is so important. Imagine! Losing his parcel. It's unthinkable. We could lose our jobs. And be the talk of the whole village!"

Bill put a comforting hand on her shoulder. "Well, I'm truly sorry, Helen, if I'm to blame. But this is Beauty Bank. People are honest and kind here. A villager has probably found it and is handing it in at the Post Office even now."

"Oh, I do hope you're right, Bill. We're certainly having no luck finding it ourselves. So, let's go back and pray it's turned up? Otherwise, I'll have to break some very unwelcome news to Mr Winstanley – and that's not something I look forward to at all."

As the couple moved away, Jack heard a caw–caw and a flutter as Rose the magpie dropped on to a branch beside him.

"Coo-er," said the bird. "Those humans are in a flap. Did you hear how they're fussing about whatever it is they've lost?"

"I did", said Jack. "In fact, Uncle Olivier sent me up to scout but, sorry, I can't stop now to chat. We're incredibly busy... waiting."

"Waiting? Waiting for what?"

"To be honest, I'm not sure. Waiting and watching, my uncle says – with peanuts."

Rose's black eyes glittered hungrily. "Peanuts, eh? That's interesting. And would you happen to know where these peanuts are?"

"Of course – they're on the grass there, near the shiny silver... foil.

Before Jack could finish, Rose was up and off – zooming towards Rachel, Uncle Olivier and a small glittering square on which rested two tasty-looking examples of her most favourite food of all.

The magpie circled once, twice and was just lining up for her final approach when – thud! A big bumble bee buzzed smack into her face leaving Rose feeling as if she had been thumped by a fluffy yellow and black pillow.

"Oops," said Uncle Olivier, observing the mid-air collision. "Stand by for a crash landing".

Above the mice, a dazed Rose was flapping frantically, trying to regain her balance, and squawking in alarm as the ground got closer.

But eventually she landed (rather more clumsily than usual), grumbling: "Pah! Bumble bees. Nothing that fat should be allowed in the air."

"But the good thing is that you've arrived now, Rose, unhurt" said Uncle Olivier. "And I take it from your rush to get here that you've seen the treat we've laid out."

He nodded towards the peanuts, adding: "And when you've eaten those, we'd very much like a chat about a small problem we're having... and how you can enjoy even more peanuts if you'll help."

****

Back in Beauty Bank, the gentle "ting" of a brass bell announced the return of Helen and Bill to the Post Office. Usually, every arrival was sure to get a cheerful smile from Anne, the Post Office assistant. But, today, she was looking just as unhappy as the two people entering.

"Oh dear," said Helen. "That look tells me our prayers haven't been answered – no one's called, then, with a parcel to hand in?"

"No," said Anne. "But Mr Winstanley has been in, complaining there's still no sign of his parcel and demanding an explanation. He wants you to phone him as soon as you get back. And he's very steamed up, I'm afraid."

Helen felt suddenly light-headed, and clutched at a rotary magazine rack for support – sending it spinning wildly and spilling out several glossy magazines. "Typical!" she groaned. "Can this day get any worse?"

Bill was bending to help her to pick up the fallen items when Helen shocked him by snapping: "Leave it. You've done quite enough as it is" – the first unkind words he'd ever heard her say.

Seeing Bill's hurt look, Helen remembered he was also worried and in a softer voice said: "Really, Bill, your shift ended ages ago. You should go home." But Bill was so upset, he stormed out, slamming the door so hard the little brass door bell fell off, with a
'ring, ting, ding' to the floor.

"Mmmm. Tasty," cooed Rose, as she carefully peeled the dry papery skin from her second peanut and gobbled down the kernel inside. "And you've got more nuts, you say, to trade for a bit of help? Sounds fair. So, let'shear it, then. What's your problem?"

Despite many interruptions from Jack, including "snow storm", "Indians", "ambush", "and "flying objects", Uncle Olivier filled Rose in on the events of the morning, starting with Bill the postman's fall on the bridge.

At the end of the explanation, Rose gave a nod: "Okay! So, to sum up – parcel lost, parcel found, stuck in hedge, needs rescuing, involves a job for a flier, pay is peanuts. So far so interesting – what's the rest?"

Uncle Olivier replied: "I'll come to that but first we need a volunteer to climb up and into the hedge and thread this twine through the string on the parcel and bring an end of the twine back down."

"Me, me!" said Jack, jumping with excitement. "Let me do it! I'm by far the best climber!" "And the best at getting stuck and falling over" chipped in Rachel. "And also the very worst at tying and untying laces."

Uncle Olivier knew his niece was right; young Jack did still have trouble with knots. But the old mouse had not forgotten Jack's upset earlier about missing his Mum and Dad, nor how much the youngster wanted the admiration of his parents and his sister!

"Okay, Jack. As you have bravely volunteered, we will appoint you the expedition leader".

Rachel was about to protest when Uncle Olivier quickly added: "And Rachel here will be commander-in-chief of the twine department, making sure Jack knows how to tie and untie it and loop it through the parcel."

"What about me, though?" asked Rose. "When do I get to be a boss?"

"You, Rose, will be our chief flight officer! Once Jack has attached the twine to the parcel, we will need you to grip the ends in your beak and pull with all of your might, so dragging the parcel out of the hedge and delivering it here at our feet."

"Is that when I'll get the other peanuts?" asked Rose, with an eye on the little balls of silver foil lying close to where Olivier was standing.

"Precisely," said Uncle Olivier, planting himself firmly between the bird and the treats. "So, is everyone clear about their roles?"

"Yes, sir," said Jack, standing tall and giving a smart salute. "All present and correct, sir, and ready for action."

Rachel felt a sudden strong flood of love for her baby brother. True, she could rarely resist teasing him or telling him off but she wouldn't swap him for all the cheese in the world, and was so proud that he was such a brave little chap.

She reached out to him: "Are you sure you're okay with this? It's a steep climb, and dangerous. No one will blame you if you decide you can't do it on your own."

"No, Sis, I'm fine and I won't be on my own, will I? I'll have you holding the twine at this end, keeping me safe – like always. So stop giving me that goofy look and tie me up. Onwards or upwards, remember?"

With a shy kiss to his cheek, Rachel looped the twine around Jack's waist, double-checking that it was secure and that Jack knew which end of the bow to pull when he got to the parcel.

With a grin, Jack stretched up to grasp the first thorny branch of the hedge and swung himself into the greenery. As Jack's tail disappeared amid the leaves, his uncle and the magpie were cheering: "Go, Jack go" and "Hurray".

But Jack also heard a quieter voice – his sister's, whispering: "Just you wait, little man. When Mum and Dad come back, the very first thing I'm going to tell them is that you're a hero."

To start, the climb seemed easy. The hedge's sharp thorns made useful hand and foot-holds and Rachel was unravelling the twine at a good, steady, pace.

Jack looked down and was surprised at how far he had climbed in such a short time and – with a gulp – what a very long way he was now from firm ground.

The thought made him suddenly dizzy, causing him to wobble, lose his grip, and shriek as he grabbed out in panic for a thorny branch.

"Jack!" cried Rachel. "Are you OK up there?"

"Yes", he replied, back on a safe perch, "I just need to remember not to look down".

A short while later, he called again: "Hey, you lot! I can see the parcel now."

"Can you touch it yet?" asked Uncle Olivier.

"Just a couple more branches. There! I'm above the spot now. So hold the twine as tight as you can while I swing into position and then when I say the password, let me down, very slowly."

"What password?" asked Rachel.

"Lower," said Jack, then screamed. "Aaaargh! Not yet. What are you doing?

"But you said 'lower'," shouted Rachel.

"Doh! I was telling you that 'lower' is the password – you only need to lower me when I say 'lower'".

"Well, don't blame me. You just said 'lower' three times in one breath. Make up your mind. Do you want lowering yet or not."

"All right, all right. Let's try it properly now. Lower!"

Uncle Olivier joined Rachel at gripping the twine, ready to support Jack's weight. Then – whoosh – Jack was lifted off his final branch and swinging freely in mid air. "Wheeeee," he yelled. "This is fun."

"Terrific," grunted Rachel. "But can you get a move on? You're really quite heavy for us to hold up."

"Yes," said Uncle Olivier. "Onwards or upwards, my boy!"

"Actually", Rachel corrected him. "That would be completely the wrong way. Jack needs to be heading down this time".

"Oh dear, so he does. Right then, young Jack. Onwards and downwards it is."

Mr Winstanley
Church Street

Moments later, Jack felt himself dropping – but, alarmingly, starting to spin as well. He stretched out his feet, trying desperately to get a toehold on the parcel. Then, with one giant step – for a mouse, that is – he landed on the surface of the parcel.

Soon, holding on to the white string for support, he was walking carefully towards the centre of the package. From there, he reported, wearily: "Okay. I've made it to where the string crosses over. What now, Base Camp?"

"Hurray," came the cheers from the ground and, from Rachel: "Well done, bro. Now, make sure you're fastened on safely, then take a little rest, while we sort out what we need to do next."

Within two ticks, the exhausted adventurer was fastened in place and beginning a much-needed sleep.

Meanwhile, Rachel was talking to her uncle in an urgent whisper. "I'm worried. Is there enough baling twine left in the ball to bring Jack safely all the way back down?"

With much pulling, pointing and pacing back and forth, the ball of twine was inspected until Uncle Olivier finally announced: "Yes. It is long enough. Just."

"But," he went on, "the next part of the operation is even trickier so I recommend that we all freshen up with a nibble and a nap."

Rachel knew her uncle was right but she felt much too wound up to sleep. Her little brother was alone and far away; it wasn't clear how they'd get him and the parcel down and they still hadn't worked out what to do with the parcel once they had got it the ground.

So while her uncle snoozed and Rose flew off to find herself food and a place to perch, Rachel sat staring across the sunlit meadow, watching how the long shadows from the tree branches danced as a breeze stirred the grass.

Amid the sounds of the breeze, birds and bees, she could hear Uncle Olivier gently snoring.

His snoring is just like him, she thought – warm, kind and comforting. And as she listened she also drifted slowly into a deep, deep, sleep.

Time passed, and Rachel was dreaming that she could hear a voice calling. It was coming from a long way off, but getting louder, and – could it be – more annoyed.

"Hedge to Base Camp, come in, over. Hello, over. Oy! Below! Uncle Olivier? Rachel? Anybody? Rachel? Rachel! RACHEL!!!"

Rachel woke with a start. Red-faced, she quickly let Jack know he hadn't been forgotten and then shook her uncle awake.

"Right," said Uncle Olivier. "We move to stage two. But, my, oh, my, where's Rose?"

He and Rachel looked all around the field, calling Rose's name, but could see no sign of the magpie anywhere.

Uncle Olivier scratched his head. "Oh dear, it looks as if Rose has forgotten us. So, time for Plan B, I think." "Plan B?" asked Rachel. "I didn't know we had a second plan that didn't involve Rose. What is it?"

"Aah," said Uncle Olivier. "Well, to be honest, I'm still working it out. But, here goes.... Jack! Are you still in the middle of the parcel?"

"Yes, uncle", replied Jack.

"Excellent. So please will you hold on tight to the string, then undo the bow Rachel tied at your waist?"

"Okay. Doing it now", came a voice from above.

"Good lad. Now, I want you to tug up plenty of spare twine, pass the loose end under the parcel string and then tie the twine tightly to the string. But make sure you're holding on, and don't forget to leave enough twine over for it to go back around your waist. Understand?"
"Got you. Starting now."

Rachel hardly dared to breathe as the sounds from inside the hedge showed that Jack was struggling to keep his balance and tie a good firm knot.

Moments later, she let out a 'phew' when Jack called down: "Operation completed" only to suck it in again when Uncle Olivier cried: "Steady boy."

"Don't move yet! Is the twine back around your waist, and have you checked that it is secure?" "Oops," they heard, followed by some scrabbling and eventually an "All done, uncle!"

Uncle Olivier was so delighted he danced a little jig, shouting: "Excellent job. What a very exciting mission this is turning out to be!"

In the Post Office, Helen took a deep breath while waiting for her call to Mr Winstanley to be answered. But at the click, all she got was a recorded greeting, an invitation to "please leave a message after the tone" and a bleep.

Helen was glad not to have to talk to Mr Winstanley in person. Even so, she was nervous as she told the recording device: "It's Helen here, from the Post Office. Sorry I missed you this morning but I just wanted to say that we're still looking for... I mean.... still looking into why your parcel hasn't been delivered and will contact you again as soon as we hear."

Helen was replacing the handset with a sigh when she was startled by a voice from the other side of the counter.

"Lost something, Helen?" It was Mrs Green from the store next door. Helen ignored the question. "Oh, hello, Mrs Green. How can I help?

"Not me, dear – the Vicar. He just popped into my shop with extra raffle tickets for tomorrow's May Fair but he was in such a rush to visit Mr Winstanley, I offered to call round with yours."

"Thanks," said Helen, with a troubled frown. "But why does the Vicar need to see Mr Winstanley so urgently?" "Well, it's so exciting, isn't it? I'd have thought we all wanted to see the lovely surprise Mr Winstanley has arranged?"

"A surprise? From Mr Winstanley?" Helen gulped, to hide the thought that had just entered her head. "I'm sorry – what surprise?"

Mrs Green paused. "That's odd. I'm sure the Vicar said Mr Winstanley was expecting it to be delivered by post this morning. So I thought you'd know all about it."

"No." Helen gulped again. "Go on. This surprise – did the Vicar say what it is?"

"Oh yes. A lovely new sparkling tiara – for tomorrow's crowning of the May Queen. It seems that when they got the old one out at the rehearsal, it was looking so battered and dull that Mr Winstanley immediately offered to buy a brand new one. So kind."

Giving a puzzled frown, Mrs Green continued: But I was sure you would have seen the package. Oh, well, it must be coming another way and we'll all be able see it in all its glory tomorrow, won't we? Now, then, must dash. 'Bye."

With that, Mrs Green went back to her own shop – unaware that Helen was now looking even more upset than before as it sunk in what the lost parcel contained.

Anne gave Helen a look full of worried sympathy. "Would a nice cup of tea help?" Helen groaned, putting her head in her hands. "To be honest, Anne, I think only a miracle will help us now".

Uncle Olivier was about to give Jack his instructions on how to come down when suddenly the parcel moved and Jack felt himself sliding towards its edge. He made a grab for the white string but it was too late. He was slithering faster and faster towards the long drop below.

"Help!" he squealed, sending Uncle Olivier and Rachel rushing to peer up the hedge to find out what was happening. To their horror, they could only watch helplessly as Jack slipped over the parcel's edge and began falling, falling into thin air...

Then, sharply, he jerked to a halt and was now bouncing above their heads like a yoyo, dangling from an end of the twine. Rachel was quick to realise what was needed. "More twine!" she shouted to her uncle. "We need to let out more twine!"

But when Uncle Olivier looked behind at where they had fixed their end of the twine to a tree stump, he shook his head.

"There isn't any more twine! Look! It is stretched out as tight as it can be!"

Rachel covered her eyes in despair while Uncle Olivier peered anxiously up at Jack who by now was spinning wildly on his thin lifeline. "Base Camp," he called down. "We have a problem!"

"You can say that again," muttered Rachel before shouting back in the calmest voice she could manage. "It's okay, Jack. Just hang on."

"But that's the problem – I am just hanging on, by a very thin thread", Jack yelled in reply. "And it's scary!"

Rachel turned to Uncle Olivier and suggested: "What if I climb the hedge until I can grab hold of his line and pull it over until he can get hold of a branch and climb down?"

"It's a brave thought, Rachel," Uncle Olivier agreed. "But look where he is. There isn't a branch within reach and the chances are that you will both get stuck – or fall a very long way. We need to come up with a safer way." Anxious seconds ticked by as Uncle Olivier paced up and down, thinking hard, and Rachel fought to stop crying.

Then, just as both thought all was lost, there was a flutter of wings by their side, and a beady eye and a beak blocking their view.

"You still got those peanuts?" asked Rose the magpie.

"Did you miss me? I flew a bit further off than I intended."

"Oh, Rose!" said Rachel, clapping her paws together. "You've come back at just the right time. Look! Jack's stuck. Please, oh, please will you help him get down!"

With just a few flaps of her powerful wings, Rose soared high into the hedge, landed near to where Jack was dangling and reached out to grasp the belt of twine around Jack's waist with her clawed right foot. Then with graceful power, she pulled back, taking Jack on the twine with her.

"Wow" yelled Jack as Rose hauled him into the air. "This is amazing. I'm flying."

The twine now ran all the way from a tree stump at Base Camp to a point high in the hedge, through the string around the parcel, then down to where it circled Jack's waist.

And with one low swoop, Rose dropped Jack gently on to the grassy bank before soaring out across the meadow.

But as Jack rolled on his back, he saw that he still wasn't out of danger. The tugs from Rose had also freed the parcel from the hedge – and it was now falling straight towards him.

He shut his eyes tight, and waited to be squashed flat. But no impact came. Instead, the twine snagged, bringing the parcel to a sudden stop so that it was now bouncing just above his nose, as if it was on an elastic band.

"Gosh. That was fun!" said Jack as Rachel fussed around, untying knots, hugging and kissing him and generally being very embarrassing.

Meanwhile, Uncle Olivier was showering Rose with praise and thanks, hardly noticing that Rose's beady eyes were busily looking everywhere except at him.

"Yeah, yeah, happy to help. But what about my peanuts?"

"Oh, but, of course, Rose." Rachel told the magpie with a sunny smile. "They're in the foil by the tree stump. Please help yourself. You deserve them." "Too right," said Jack, now back on his feet. "But can I just point out that we're not quite finished yet. The parcel still hasn't landed."

Three mousy groans made Rose look up from pecking at her peanuts to check the latest problem. "Okay, guys, stand back," she said and with a couple of pecks of her razor sharp beak snapped the twine near the tree stump, causing the parcel to fall to the ground with a thud.

"Rose, you're a marvel," said Uncle Olivier. "Of course, we still need to get the parcel back to its owner but I'm sure we'll solve that challenge just as soon as we've all had a good night's sleep.... I mean... think."

In truth, they all knew that returning the parcel would be an even bigger problem than the ones they had already solved. But they were too tired and hungry for any more adventures.

So as Rose flew away, the three little mice made their way back to their tree house home and by the time darkness crept across the meadow, each and every one of them was fast asleep.

****

When the first shotgun blast rang out across the fields of Hall Farm, Uncle Olivier woke with a start. When the second shot cracked the morning air, both Rachel and Jack were jerked from their sleep too.

"Oh dear" said Uncle Olivier. "It sounds as if Kevin the fox has been up to no good in the henhouse again. It's just as well he's fast and cunning – and that the farmer is too mean to buy himself a new pair of glasses!"

"But don't you wish Kevin would stop going after those poor chickens. I feel so sorry for them," said Rachel.

"True," said Uncle Olivier, walking to the door and breathing deeply. "But it could be worse. Kevin might decide he liked eating mice instead".

Rachel was still shuddering at the thought of being fox food when Uncle Olivier added: "Talking of which.... Kevin seems to be heading our way" – prompting a worried Rachel and Jack to scurry out of sight.

Uncle Olivier, however, simply chuckled. "Have no fear, children. Kevin will never harm us. I sheltered him here when he was a tiny cub being chased by the hunt. We're old friends."

A heavy panting outside the den signalled the fox's arrival.

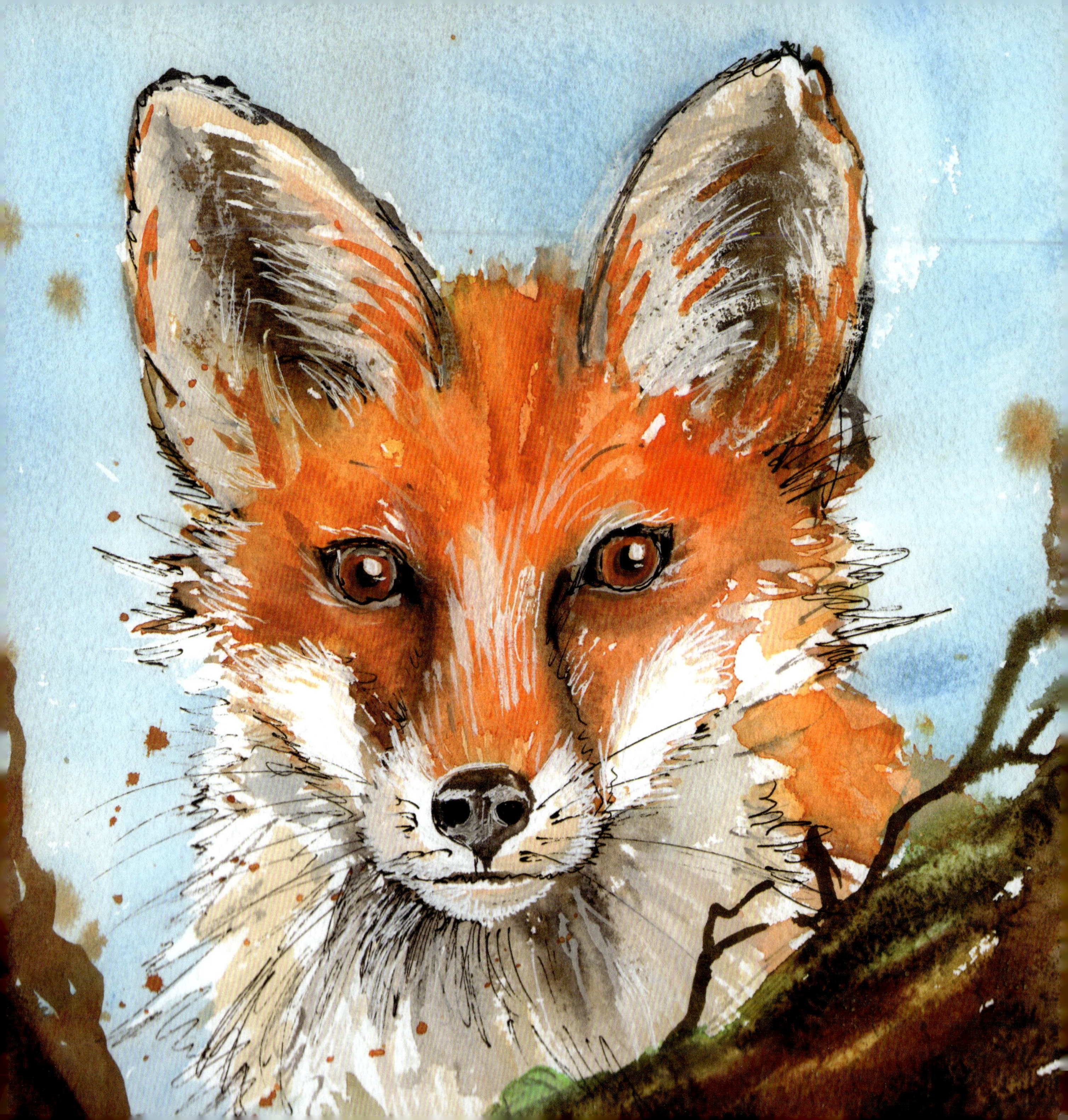

"Morning, Kevin!" said Uncle Olivier cheerfully. "Aren't you getting a bit too old for all this running about?"

Kevin growled: "Huh! I'm not on my last legs yet, little mouse, and I wouldn't have to run at all but for the noisy racket those silly chickens make every time I get anywhere near their coop."

"Gracious!" laughed Uncle Olivier. "Hens upset about a fox? Whatever are they thinking?"

Kevin chuckled back as he lay down on the warm grass beside the doorway. "It beats me. But it's very tiring dodging the farmer's gun just to get a snack, so if it's all the same with you, I'll use this sunny spot of yours for a doze." And, with that, the fox stretched out and closed his eyes.

Nervously, Rachel joined her uncle in the doorway and looked out at Kevin sleeping. Despite her sympathies for chickens, she could not help but admire the rich ginger-red of Kevin's fur and how the sun picked out its golden highlights.

It struck her as strange that, asleep, Kevin looked gentle enough to pat even though she knew he had fierce teeth, strong jaws and the powerful body of a fast runner.

All at once, an idea came to her. In a low voice, she asked: "Uncle Olivier, would Kevin be good at carrying?"

Uncle Olivier was puzzled. "Carrying what, my dear?"

"The parcel!" said Rachel, still whispering. "I'm wondering if Kevin could carry the package into the village."

But even the smallest sounds don't escape the sharp ears of a fox, even one that appears to be asleep. "What parcel, and where's it got to go," asked Kevin lazily, with a yawn.

Helen was catching up on paperwork in the back room of the Post Office when her assistant Anne called: "Can you come through, Helen? Mr Winstanley is here."

"Oh, no," groaned Helen to herself, before calling back "Okay. I'm on my way" and trying hard to put a smile of welcome on her face.

At the counter, Mr Winstanley did not look pleased. "Anne tells me there is a problem with the parcel I was expecting yesterday but which still hasn't been delivered."

"Quite so," said Helen, wishing the floor would open and swallow her up. "The problem is, Mr Winstanley, and I'm very, very, sorry to say it, but your parcel is... well... missing."

"Missing!" shouted Mr Winstanley "But how, and where. And what are you doing to find it?"

"We're looking everywhere, I promise", said Helen. "The thing is that I'm certain it left here on Friday morning but Bill had an accident on his bike and a lot of items fell out of his bag. He was sure he collected everything up but... well... we haven't seen your parcel since."

"Well, this is terrible," said Mr Winstanley. "It's vital we find the parcel at once. It contains a very expensive tiara – the tiara that I have promised will be available for this afternoon's crowning of the new May Queen!"

"I know," said Helen unhappily. "But we've searched everywhere. I don't know what else to do or say. I'm deeply sorry".

"No doubt," snapped Mr Winstanley, "but not quite as sorry as I will be when I have to explain why, despite my promise, the May Queen will today receive a crown so old and battered, it is more suited to the head of a scarecrow!"

Helen started to sob as Mr Winstanley turned sharply to leave, slamming shut the door. Anne passed Helen a tissue to dry her tears and tried to find some words of comfort.

"Don't get too upset, Helen. Even if the parcel doesn't turn up in time, the May Queen can still be crowned with the old tiara. It may be old, and a bit bent, and missing most of its diamantes, but I doubt anyone will notice... at least not from a distance."

Helen gave a small smile. "But it's the embarrassment, Anne, and the disappointment. The whole village would be so thrilled to see the May Queen in a sparkling new tiara. And what will people think of me? My reputation will be in ruins..."

With this thought, Helen's tears welled up again, prompting her to grab the box of tissues and dash into the back room – just in time to avoid a grand entrance by Mrs Green.

"Well, well," the shopkeeper said to Anne, wagging a finger. "You kept that very quiet!"

"Kept what quiet, Mrs Green?" said Anne.

"Oh, don't pretend. Mr Winstanley has just told me all about the loss of the parcel containing the tiara."

Anne was about to explain that all Post Office business was confidential when a loud sob came from the room behind her. So she decided, instead, to beg a favour.

"Listen, Mrs Green! Can't you hear? Helen is breaking her heart over this. I know you always like to be the one who knows everything that's happening in the village and pass it around. But, please, for once, will you help us to keep this quiet? We're doing everything we can to find the parcel and there's still time for a miracle."

"Hrrrmph," said Mrs Green, recognising that as much as she was fond of juicy gossip, she never meant to be deliberately unkind.

"Well, I suppose I can keep it to myself for now. But, mark my words, there was a magpie on your roof and you know what that means – sorrow's coming. And, personally, I don't believe in miracles."

The sun was now beaming down upon the streets of Beauty Bank, catching on the garlands of brightly-coloured flags and bunting hanging between lamp posts and on railings.

There were busy scenes all around as grown-ups marked the route of the parade, set up stalls, added flower arrangements to the stage for the crowning ceremony, and lined up decorated floats, ready for the procession. In other places, excited children were putting on their carnival costumes or eyeing the fairground games they wanted to try out first.

In short, it looked to be the start of a joyful day. But as Helen looked out of the post office window the cheerful sights only added to the heavy feeling in her heart.

All these villagers looking forward to seeing the village May Queen in a new sparkling tiara, she thought sadly, yet none of them realising that the lovely new crown is nowhere to be found.

A warm breeze was sweeping across the meadow by the time Uncle Olivier had finished telling Kevin the story of their discovery – and heroic rescue – of a parcel needed urgently in the village.

"I'd best have a look at it, then," said Kevin, fixing his glossy brown eyes on Rachel, so close she could see herself reflected in their shine. "Fancy a ride, little miss? You can steer me to it."

Now, accepting a lift on the back of a fox with a strong appetite for smaller creatures wasn't exactly how Rachel wanted to start her day. But Kevin's smile seemed friendly enough and she didn't want Jack to be the family's only hero.

So she swallowed her fears and scurried up a ginger wall of fur on to Kevin's back. "Who's the cowboy now?" she called down to Jack as she rode away – not noticing that her brother was staring speechless at her daring.

Travelling by fox turned out to be more fun than Rachel expected and so fast that they reached the parcel in no time. Kevin stretched his front legs forwards to let Rachel down on to the grass and soon both were examining the find.

By grasping the soft white string, Rachel pulled herself up onto the top of the box for a closer look at the small sticker in one corner showing a picture of a queen.

Meanwhile, Kevin was sniffing around the edges, giving the box the occasional nudge with his nose. One of his pushes caught Rachel off guard, causing her to lose her balance and fall bottom-first on to the Queen's head.

"Sorry, Your Majesty", she giggled, with a nod at the sticker, but stopped and gasped as she saw Kevin heading towards her, with his jaws wide open, revealing two rows of razor-sharp teeth.

But, just as she feared she was about to be eaten, Kevin paused, gave her a friendly wink, and closed his teeth gently around the parcel string, before swinging both the parcel and its passenger easily into the air.

Rachel had to hold on very tightly to the string for the up-and-down trot back to the tree house, but it did mean Kevin listened closely to Rachel's every idea about what the parcel contained.

The fact is, he had no choice. He couldn't open his mouth to say "shut up" without letting go of the string AND allowing it and Rachel to fall. But as soon as they got back to the tree house, Kevin voiced an idea of his own.

"Miss Chatterbox has set me thinking. She reckons this sticker showing a queen with a crown is a clue to what is inside the box.

And that reminds me of some chitter-chatter I overheard last night when I was checking out dustbins in the village." He went on: "The story is that the Post Office has lost a package containing a new tiara, and that the tiara is needed for the crowning of the May Queen. Today. At 2pm."

Rachel gasped. "But if the crowning ceremony is today, that means we've absolutely got to get the parcel back straightaway. Imagine. How awful. To be a queen without a lovely crown to wear..."

"Precisely," said Uncle Olivier. "So, has anyone got any suggestions on the next move?"

"Maybe", said Kevin. "The crowning ceremony happens in the field next to the church. But nearly everyone from the village joins or watches the procession which starts at 1.30pm. So, the field should be quiet while the procession wiggles round the village – giving us the chance to sneak on to the field, then, and drop the parcel off. Unseen. Fox-like."

"Wow", said Jack. "This adventure gets better and better!" "That's a very good suggestion, Kevin", said Uncle Olivier. "But can we get there in time? Sadly, our little legs aren't quite as long or as strong as yours."

"Oh, stop hinting, Olivier!" said Kevin. "As Rachel will tell you, journeys are faster by fox. Hop on and I'll take you there in no time."

"Me, too?" asked Jack with excitement.

"You, too," said Kevin with a toothy grin.

Helen and Anne were at the Post Office window, watching the village folk assemble in their finest clothes for the May Fair Parade. They could see Boy Scouts and Girl Guides in uniforms, fancy dress characters, cars tied with ribbons and bows, and a magnificent horse-drawn carriage for the May Queen and her attendants.

As the church clock struck 1pm, Helen couldn't stand to watch any longer, she pulled down the window blind and locked the door.

Anne gave a disappointed "oh", adding: "Don't be like that. We always join the parade and attend the fair. We can't miss it just because of one lost parcel."

Helen replied: "I suppose so. But can we stay near the back? I won't be able to bear it if people start pointing and whispering."

****

Kevin crouched down to let Rachel and Jack guide a wobbly Uncle Olivier up onto the fox's furry back. And then they were off, with Kevin firmly holding the parcel in his jaws and Jack shouting: "Wheeeeee. This is awesome!"

At a fence, Kevin tried to warn his passengers "Hold on" but it came out as mumble because he was gripping the parcel so tightly in his teeth. Fortunately, Rachel understood and shouted "Grab some fur. He's going to jump!" just before Kevin leapt gracefully across the fence and landed softly on the other side.

Keeping close to the hedgerow so as not to be seen, Kevin made his way along the side of the road towards the church.

There, they could see the parade entering the field through an archway of bright coloured flags. Spotting the last two walkers, Rachel asked: "Isn't that the lady from the Post Office – the one who came to the bridge?"

"So, it is!" replied Jack.

Rachel decided: "She's the one who needs to get the parcel, then. If we can just return it to her, I feel sure everything will turn out fine".

Uncle Olivier surveyed the fairground, noticing a small red and white striped tent tucked behind the public seating area.

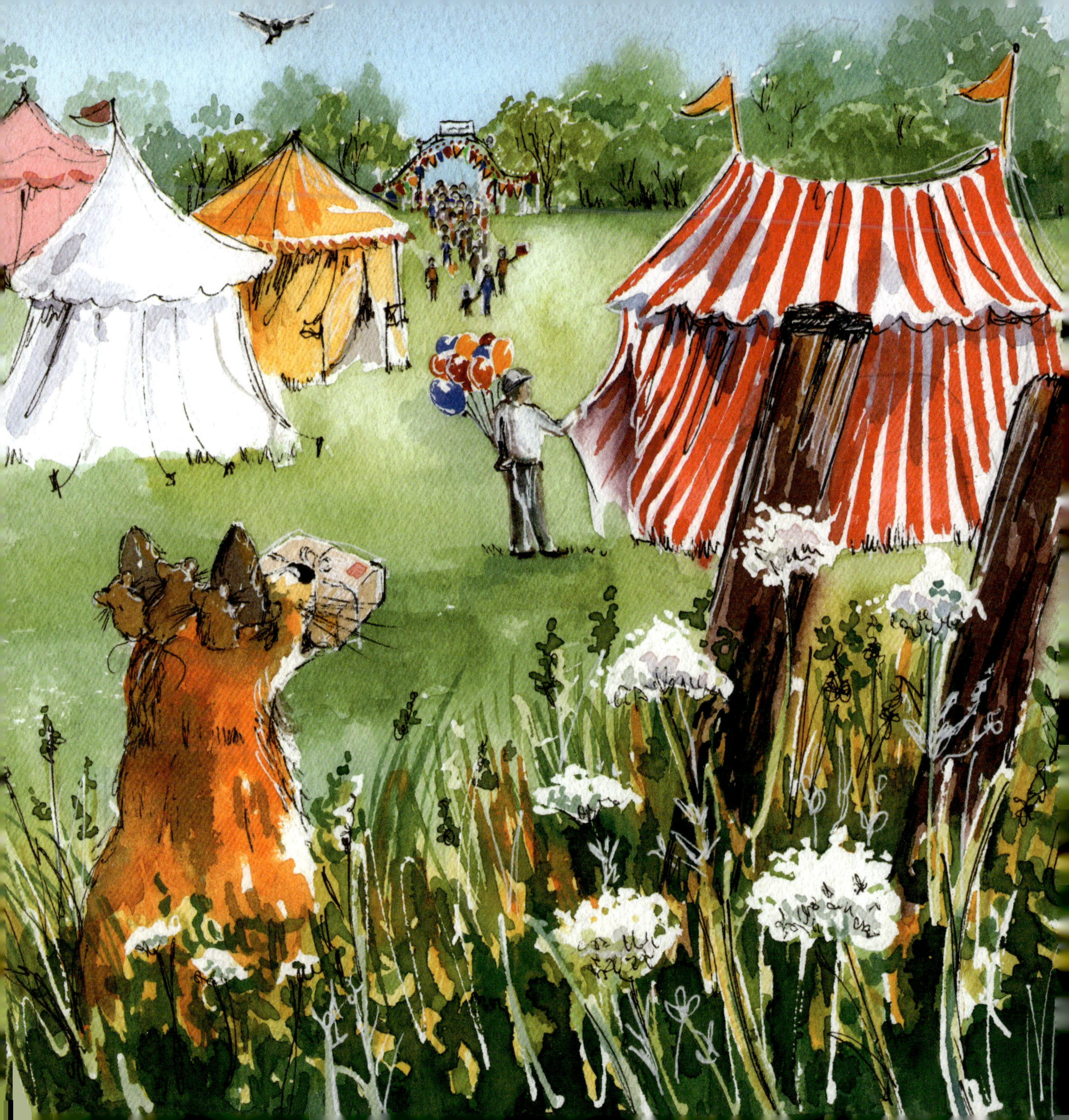

"That looks the place to hide," he suggested. Carefully, Kevin skirted the edge of the field, creeping low until he reached the rear of tent and found a gap to squeeze under.

Inside, the mice saw two chairs, tied with ribbons, and a small table covered with a long white table cloth and topped with a pink velvet cushion and a pretty posy of flowers.

Kevin let down the parcel and his passengers on the grass at the foot of the table, and then said: "If you don't mind, I think I'd better scarper now. Foxes aren't always popular with humans, you know."

After thanking Kevin warmly for all of his help, Rachel, Jack and Olivier began to look round. Suddenly, from under the table cloth they were startled to hear a small 'Psst' and to see two more mice peeking out at them.

"Carlos!" cried Jack.

"Carlos?" queried Rachel, raising her eyebrows.

"Si, I eez Carlos. The amigo of Jack from when we eez both hiding from the cat who eez named Alfie. Hola, Jack! Que pasa?"

"It's all going great, thanks... I mean... gracias."

Next, Carlos took Rachel's paw and giving a deep bow, said: "Y you must be la hermosa hermana ... sorry, the beautiful sister of Jack: Rachel!"

Then he bowed again to Uncle Olivier. "Y you eez el tio Olivier el sabio, that eez, the Wise. I eez enchanted! Now, pleez also to let me introduce to you another great amiga, Leez."

"Leez?" queried Rachel, raising her eyebrows even higher.

"It's Liz, actually," said the second mouse. "You have to excuse my friend Carlos, he's Spanish, he speaks funny. Are you all here for the cake, then? I've been telling Carlos – wherever there's cake and people, there are yummy cake crumbs for mice!"

Just then, voices from outside sent all five mice scurrying back under the table cloth. Moments later, a lady and gentleman entered, accompanied by two little girls dressed in pretty pink dresses – a perfect match for the flowers on the table and ribbons on the chairs.

The man passed a battered cardboard box to the lady, saying sadly: "This is what we'll be using for the crowning. A pity, but we have no option."

From the box, the lady lifted a dull and tarnished tiara, dotted with gray holes where once there had been sparkling diamantes and, with a sigh of disappointment, placed it on the velvet cushion.

Carlos nudged Jack with his elbow. "This man he eez Señor Winstanley. He eez very sad. He planned a beautiful new crown for Queen of the May today but the office of the post – it lose hiz parcel".

Before Jack could reply, Mr Winstanley and the lady began reminding the maids of honour about their duties and asked them to wait until they heard the music giving the signal for them bring the tiara, the cushion and the bouquet to the stage for the crowning ceremony.

"We'll pop out now to check the timings", said the lady.

"Just sit here quietly and wait for the fanfare."

"Well, that's no use," protested Rachel. "If they stay where they are, we'll never be able to return the parcel to the post lady and the queen won't get to wear the beautiful new tiara."

"Ssshhh!" said Liz. "They'll hear you. And we'll have no chance of cake if we attract attention and have to run away."

"Hang on, though," said Uncle Olivier. "That's given me a rather brilliant idea. Because if we CAN attract attention, perhaps we can get the parcel's owners to run to us."

"Que? I eez confused." said Carlos."What has the small mice to do with parcels?"

"No time for that now," said Uncle Olivier. "You boys pop out and see if the lady from the Post Office is anywhere near."

Quick as they could Carlos and Jack ran to the doorway and returned to report. "Yes. The Post Office ladies are sitting just outside with cups of tea." "Excellent", said Uncle Olivier. "So the next question is – what can five small mice do to make the humans take notice?"

Everyone thought for a while. Then Rachel said: "Jack. Do you remember me telling you that the most embarrassing day of my life was when Mum and Dad got stuck on the boat that took them away......"

"And the lady saw them, screamed and fell off the gang-plank into the river!" said Jack, catching on instantly. "Oh, yes, sis, that's a brilliant idea."

Uncle Olivier looked stern. "To be frank, it is a shocking plan". But then he gave a wide smile and added: "But shock is what we need so it's shockingly good, too."

In whispers, the boat story was explained to the others, finishing with Uncle Olivier saying: "Right, then – Jack and Carlos, you come with me to push the parcel into position while Rachel and Liz get going on Operation Mouse Fright."

On his nod, Rachel and Liz ran out from under the table skipping, squeaking and dancing around the chair legs, underneath the little girls.

Uncle Olivier and the boys had just got the parcel by the side of the chair, when they stood stock still. Instead of the screams they expected, they were hearing hand–claps of delight and laughter!

Liz had tripped over a chair leg on to her back and one of the two little girls was standing over her, cooing: "Oh, sweet! Look at the pretty little mouse! She's so cute!"

"Oops," said Jack, still frozen to the spot. "That wasn't in the plan."
"Oops, indeed," said Uncle Olivier. "Now what?"

Meanwhile, Rachel had seen Liz fall and scurried over the shiny black shoe of the other girl in her haste to help.

The second girl looked at her foot, gasped, then jumped up on her chair, screaming "Mouse! Mouse!"

The scream startled Rachel and Liz so much both they looked for the quickest way to get back behind the table cloth – a route which took them up and over two pairs of pretty, white, lace-patterned ankle socks!

Finding a mouse climbing her sock startled the first flower girl so much she also leapt on to her chair and joined in the noisy screaming so that both girls were now yelling "Mice, mice" at the top of their lungs.

Near the tent's entrance, Helen and Anne had just settled down to enjoy a cup of tea and a cake each when they heard the screams of the little girls.

So, still clutching their teacups and plates, ran inside the tent to investigate.

After shooing the children out, Helen went to the table to see what had so frightened the girls. There, she stumbled against an obstacle on the ground, causing her plate to tip and sending her iced fairy cake sliding off her plate on to the grassy floor.

Looking down to see what had caused her trip, she could hardly believe her eyes. There on the floor, next to the cake, was the missing parcel! Helen bent to it, calling: "Anne! Quick. Just look what I've found here." And the two women were still staring in astonishment when Mr Winstanley arrived, puffing: "Is there something wrong?" he asked.

"Quite the opposite," said Helen with a smile and a downwards point of her finger. "This, I believe, is yours!"

Mr Winstanley gave a delighted laugh as he took hold of the parcel and began to tear off the brown paper wrapping to reach a smart red box. Raising its lid, he then parted several crisp sheets of white tissue paper to reveal the contents - a glittering, shimmering tiara fit for a fairy–tale princess.

Rachel watched on in awe as the light caught the clever twists of golden wire, shining with crystal, pearl and beads, and imagined what it would feel like if only she could be crowned as May Queen.

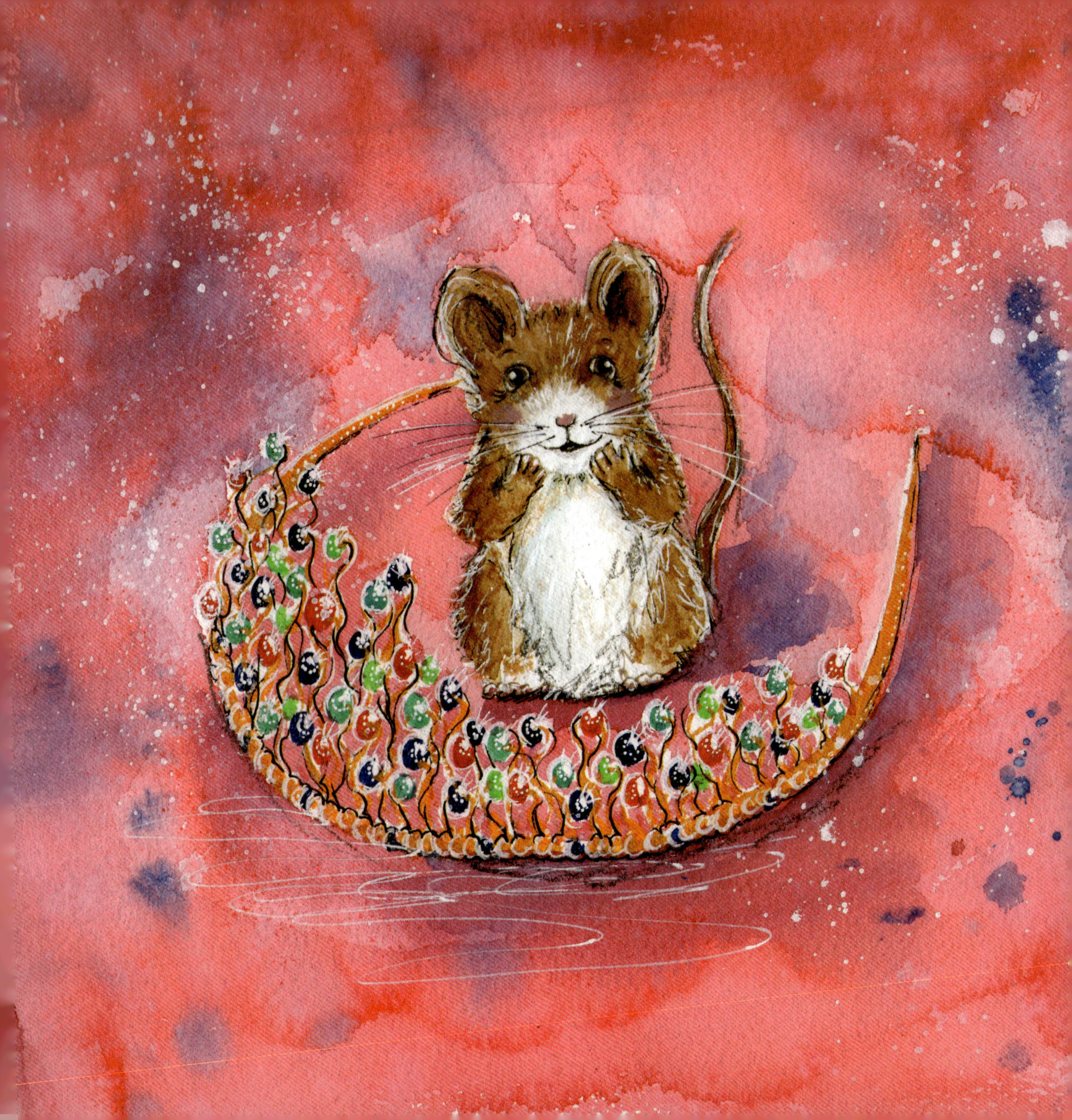

Helen, Anne and Mr Winstanley were still laughing and crying with happiness at their delightful discovery when Mrs Green arrived, demanding "Is something happening in here that I should know about?"

Anne spoke for everyone: "Only a miracle, Mrs Green. Only a miracle!"

The rest of the fete day turned out to be a huge success, with all of the villagers agreeing as they left that this year's Beauty Bank May Queen looked especially beautiful in her sparkling new tiara.

"Right then, home time, I think," said Uncle Olivier, looking around hopefully for signs of a taxi – Kevin!

But Kevin was nowhere to be found, so after saying goodbye to Liz and Carlos, the three little field mice walked leisurely across the fields towards the stone bridge and their den – each with a little lump of tasty fairy cake.

Rachel also carried a souvenir she thought even more special – a coil of white string from the parcel, soon to become her new skipping rope.

THE END

If you have enjoyed reading this story,
you may also like to read the first book in the Tales from Beauty Bank series:

"Lost in the Snow"

In this story, we join: Rachel, Jack and Uncle Olivier
as they take shelter from a snowstorm in a small village theatre.
Very soon an exciting adventure unfolds which will have you sitting on the edge of your seat.

To obtain a copy:

www.beautybankpublishing.com